MATH IN THE REAL WORLD

How Race Car Drivers Use Math

By Sheri L. Arroyo

Math Curriculum Consultant: Rhea A. Stewart, M.A.,
Specialist in Mathematics, Science,
and Technology Education

CHELSEA
CLUBHOUSE
An Imprint of Chelsea House Publishers

Math in the Real World: How Race Car Drivers Use Math

Chelsea Clubhouse
An imprint of Chelsea House Publishers
132 West 31st Street
New York NY 10001

Library of Congress Cataloging-in-Publication Data
Arroyo, Sheri L.
        How race car drivers use math / by Sheri L. Arroyo; math curriculum consultant, Rhea A. Stewart.
            p. cm. — (Math in the real world)
        Includes index.
        ISBN 978-1-60413-609-8
        1. Mathematics—Juvenile literature. 2. Automobile racing drivers—Juvenile literature.
        I. Title. II. Series.
    QA135.6.A78 2010
    510—dc22   2009021476

Chelsea Clubhouse books are available at special discounts when purchased in bulk quantities for businesses, associations, institutions, or sales promotions. Please call our Special Sales Department in New York at (212) 967-8800 or (800) 322-8755.

You can find Chelsea Clubhouse on the World Wide Web at http://www.chelseahouse.com

Developed for Chelsea House by RJF Publishing LLC (www.RJFpublishing.com)
Text and cover design by Tammy West/Westgraphix LLC
Illustrations by Spectrum Creative Inc.
Photo research by Edward A. Thomas
Index by Nila Glikin
Cover printed by Bang Printing, Brainerd, MN
Book printed and bound by Bang Printing, Brainerd, MN
Date printed: January 2011

Photo Credits: 4, 21, 22: Getty Images; 6: JASON REED/Reuters/Landov; 8: © Wm. Baker/GhostWorx Images/Alamy; 10: © Tony Watson/Alamy; 12: RUSSELL LABOUNTY/CSM/Landov; 14, 25: AP/Wide World Photos; 16: TIM WIMBORNE/Reuters/Landov; 18: ALESSANDRO BIANCHI/Reuters/Landov; 20: PAULO WHITAKER/Reuters /Landov; 24, 26: AFP/Getty Images.

Table of Contents

Answers and helpful hints for the You Do the Math
activities are in the Answer Key.

Words that are defined in the Glossary are
in **bold** type the first time they appear in the text.

Racing and Math

The drivers have suited up and climbed into their cars. Engines roar. All eyes are on the checkered flag. The flag drops. The drivers roar off—challenging themselves, their teams, and other drivers to perform to the best of their ability. Math is used by the drivers, by their pit crews, and by race car designers before, during, and after a race. This is a sport where everything is measured and **analyzed**!

The Math of Racing

There are different kinds of racing. Each has a different kind of car and

Cars race around the track at the Talladega Superspeedway.

track. In all of the types, though, math is used in many ways. How much fuel should be put in the car before a race? How fast was the driver's **qualifying time**, and how does it compare to the times of other drivers? What was the driver's speed on the straight part of the track compared with the curves? The driver and team answer these questions and more by doing math.

You Do the Math

Fastest Times

Before races on an oval track, drivers who want to compete in the race take 2 laps to drive as fast as they can. The amount of time it takes a driver to complete his fastest lap is his official qualifying time. How fast each driver went as he raced around the track is his qualifying speed. The **bar graph** shows the fastest (best) qualifying speeds recorded at 10 tracks in the years 2000–2008. Use the graph to answer the questions.

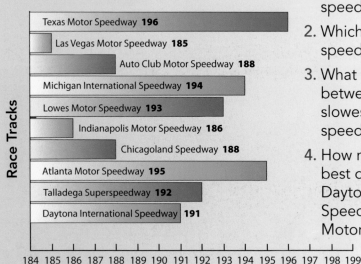

Texas Motor Speedway **196**
Las Vegas Motor Speedway **185**
Auto Club Motor Speedway **188**
Michigan International Speedway **194**
Lowes Motor Speedway **193**
Indianapolis Motor Speedway **186**
Chicagoland Speedway **188**
Atlanta Motor Speedway **195**
Talladega Superspeedway **192**
Daytona International Speedway **191**

Race Tracks

184 185 186 187 188 189 190 191 192 193 194 195 196 197 198 199

Qualifying Speeds (in miles per hour, MPH)

1. Which track's best qualifying speed was fastest?

2. Which track's best qualifying speed was slowest?

3. What is the **difference** between the fastest and slowest best qualifying speeds?

4. How much slower was the best qualifying speed at Daytona International Speedway than at Texas Motor Speedway?

Track Design

There are special tracks for different kinds of races. NASCAR races take place on oval tracks, such as the Indianapolis Motor Speedway. In NASCAR races, the cars look very much like regular cars. NASCAR stands for the National Association for **Stock Car** Auto Racing.

A view from the air of the Indianapolis Motor Speedway.

Drag racing, or hot-rod racing, is a short but fast race between two cars at a time. Drag racing is held at special tracks with a $\frac{1}{4}$-mile-long straight path for the cars to race on.

Indy Car races and Formula One races use extremely fast, specially designed race cars. Indy cars race on oval tracks. Formula One races are held on road courses.

Track Types

Oval tracks are grouped by their length. The length of a track is the distance around the track once, beginning and ending at a starting line. Short tracks are oval tracks that are less than 1 mile in length. Intermediate tracks are from 1 mile to 2 miles in length. Superspeedways are tracks greater than 2 miles in length.

Road courses are not oval in shape. They have irregular shapes and many turns (something like an actual road with many sharp curves). They are more than 2 miles long.

You Do the Math

Comparing Tracks

Look at the table with **data** about different oval tracks. The table tells how long each track is and how many people it can seat.

Data about Oval Tracks		
Track	**Length**	**Seats**
Dover	1.0 miles	140,000
Daytona Beach	2.5 miles	168,000
Charlotte	1.5 miles	165,000
Indianapolis	2.5 miles	250,000
Kansas City	1.5 miles	82,000
Martinsville	0.5 miles	65,000

1. Order the race tracks by spectator seats from the track that has the least number of seats to the track that has the greatest number.

2. Which tracks are superspeedways?

3. What is the difference in length between Daytona Beach and Martinsville?

4. Indianapolis has sold 135,000 seats for an upcoming race. How many seats are still available?

Drag Racing

A drag race is a contest between two race cars that is held on a track called a drag strip. The cars drive $\frac{1}{4}$ of a mile straight down the track. After a car crosses the finish line, the driver releases a parachute, which helps bring the car to a stop.

A drag race event will often have many cars entered in it. As each two-car race is run, the losing car is eliminated. Each winning car keeps racing until only one car is left that hasn't lost a race. That car is the winner of the event.

Elapsed Time, Speed, and Reaction Time

A race begins with a signal from an electronic device called a Christmas tree. The device has different colored lights. When the green light goes on, the race begins.

As each car takes off, it crosses a line and starts an **elapsed-time** clock. The clock stops when that car crosses the finish line. The start-to-finish

The device used to signal the start of a drag race is called a Christmas tree.

time is the car's elapsed time. The car with the shortest elapsed time wins the race. Each car's speed is also measured in a 66-foot stretch that ends at the finish line.

Speed is important to win a race, but so is the driver's reaction time. This is how quickly the driver reacts to the green light. A driver with a slower speed can still win the race if he had the fastest reaction to the green light and got his car to accelerate (pick up speed) faster at the beginning of the race.

You Do the Math

Who Wins?

The tables below show the elapsed time and the speed in miles per hour (mph) for two races. Use the tables to answer the questions.

Results of Race #1		
Driver	**Elapsed Time**	**Speed**
Steph	8.35 seconds	181.48 mph
Tran	8.09 seconds	181.45 mph

Results of Race #2		
Driver	**Elapsed Time**	**Speed**
Jason	7.68 seconds	192.51 mph
Ed	9.18 seconds	107.88 mph

1. In Race #1, which driver had the shortest elapsed time? Who had the fastest speed? Who won the race? How do you know?

2. In Race #2, who lost the race? What was the difference between his elapsed time and the winner's elapsed time?

E.T. Racing

One popular type of drag racing is called E.T. (elapsed time) racing. In this kind of racing, any two cars can race against each other. The slower car is given a head start.

Calculating the Head Start

In order to figure out which car will receive the head start, each car is timed doing a few practice runs on the $\frac{1}{4}$-mile track. The drivers use those practice times to calculate how

Two cars race down a drag strip, each driver trying to achieve the shortest elapsed time.

much time they think they need to cover the track during the actual race. This time is called their "dial-in." Drivers choose their own dial-ins, but they must choose a time they think is realistic. Any driver choosing too slow a dial-in to get a bigger head start can be disqualified from the race.

Before a race, the two drivers' dial-ins are compared. The difference between the times is the amount of the head start that will be given to the slower car.

For example, Driver A chooses a dial-in of 17 seconds, and Driver B chooses a dial-in of 15 seconds. The difference is 2 seconds ($17 - 15 = 2$). So, Driver A will get a 2-second head start against Driver B.

You Do the Math

Calculating the Dial-in

To determine his dial-in, a driver does 3 practice runs. Then, he **calculates** the **average** elapsed time for these runs by adding the 3 times together and then dividing the **sum** by 3. For example, Driver C is timed at 15, 14, and 16 seconds. The average time is 15 seconds:

$$15 + 14 + 16 = 45$$
$$45 \div 3 = 15$$

He chooses 15 seconds as his dial-in. Calculate the dial-ins for these drivers, assuming each one uses the average of his practice times as his dial-in.

1. Driver D: practice runs of 12, 10, and 14 seconds
2. Driver E: practice runs of 14.5, 16, and 16 seconds

Go as Fast as You Can!

Not every race car driver who wants to compete in a NASCAR race can do so. In the days before a race, drivers and their cars must "qualify" (earn a place in the race) by performing well enough in what are called the qualifying rounds. The first step is for a member of each driver's race team to go to a drawing where a bingo-like machine gives each driver a number. The numbers tell drivers when it's their turn to try to qualify.

In the qualifying rounds, cars go around the track one at a time. After warming up, drivers have two laps to go as fast as they can. Each lap is timed separately, and the faster of

Racing fans watch the cars zip by during a NASCAR race.

the two times is the car's qualifying time. Only drivers with the faster qualifying times will get to compete in the actual race. Those with the slower times are eliminated.

Winning the Pole Position

For drivers competing in the race, qualifying time is also important in another way. It determines each car's position on the track at the start of the race. The best qualifying time gets the best starting position. That is called the **pole position**. This position is in the first row closest to the inside of the track. The best place to start the race is from the pole position.

Drivers' Records

Does the driver who starts the race from the pole position always win the race? Not necessarily. Look at the graph, which shows how often 5 drivers won the pole position (pole starts) and won races (race wins).

1. Which driver won the most races?

2. Which driver won the pole position most often?

3. How many more race wins did Driver B have than Driver D?

4. How many more pole starts did Driver D have than Driver B?

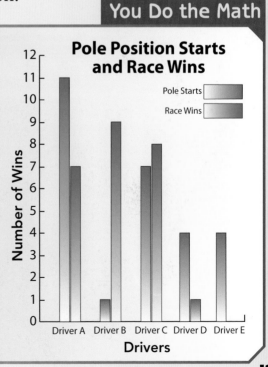

Pole Position Starts and Race Wins

Pole Starts
Race Wins

Number of Wins

Driver A Driver B Driver C Driver D Driver E

Drivers

NASCAR: Winning the Championship

During race season, there are regular NASCAR races each week for 26 weeks. Drivers earn points depending on how they place in each race. The driver finishing in first place gets the most points: 185. A second-place finish earns 170 points, and the driver finishing in third place gets 165 points. Decreasing numbers of points are earned for each place down to 43rd place, which earns 34 points. A driver can also earn 5 bonus points for leading any lap, as well as 5 more bonus points for leading the most laps during the race.

A driver celebrates in Victory Lane after winning a NASCAR race.

The Championship

At the end of the first 26 races, the sum of each driver's points is calculated. The 12 drivers with the most points are eligible for the championship. These drivers take part in 10 more races to see who will win the championship. Each driver starts with 5,000 points, plus 10 points for every race he or she won during the first part of the season. Then, points are earned in each of the 10 races to determine the champion.

You Do the Math

Adding the Points

How are these four drivers doing so far this season? The table shows the points each one earned for each of the first 4 regular races.

Driver	Race 1		Race 2		Race 3		Race 4	
	Finish Points	Bonus Points	Finish Points	Bonus Points	Finish Points	Bonus Points	Finish Points	Bonus Points
A	150	0	142	0	165	5	134	0
B	124	0	138	0	134	0	146	5
C	170	5	185	10	170	5	185	10
D	142	5	150	5	160	5	150	5

Points Earned by 4 Drivers in 4 Races

1. Calculate how many total points each driver has after 4 races.

2. How many more total points does Driver C have than Driver A?

3. Which driver has the fewest total points?

4. Which driver has earned the most bonus points?

5. Put the drivers in order from greatest to least number of total points.

Formula One

Formula One (F1) is another kind of car racing. F1 races do not take place on oval tracks. Instead, the races (there are about 18 in each year's racing season) are held on special winding tracks. About half the races are held in Europe, but F1 races take place all over the world. Drivers, too, come from many different countries. The cars look something like insects—long snouts, wing-like parts to help keep the car stable on the track, wheels entirely outside the body—and they cost many millions of dollars each.

An F1 driver speeds down the track during a practice run.

Race Strategy

Cars don't pass each other very often in F1 races because the tracks are winding and narrow. This means that teams come up with strategies for getting ahead of other cars. They calculate fuel levels, **pit stops**, choice of tires, and driving strategy for different parts of the track in order to try to be the first one to cross the finish line. There are practice and qualifying rounds on Friday and Saturday, where the drivers work to get a good starting position. Then, the race is held on Sunday. The Sunday race is called a Grand Prix.

Comparing NASCAR and Formula One

How are NASCAR and Formula One races alike? How are they different? Study the **Venn diagram** below to answer the questions.

1. How are the race track designs different in NASCAR and Formula One?
2. How is the design of a Formula One car different from the design of a NASCAR race car?
3. Name two things that are the same in NASCAR and Formula One racing.

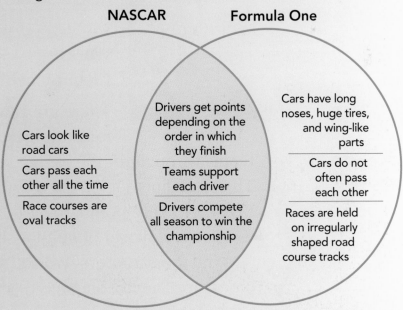

NASCAR   Formula One

Cars look like road cars

Cars pass each other all the time

Race courses are oval tracks

Drivers get points depending on the order in which they finish

Teams support each driver

Drivers compete all season to win the championship

Cars have long noses, huge tires, and wing-like parts

Cars do not often pass each other

Races are held on irregularly shaped road course tracks

F1: The Driver and His Team

Every Formula One race car is driven by a highly talented driver and is designed, built, and managed by an entire team of engineers, designers, and managers. A team is known as a "constructor." Some well-known F1 teams, or constructors, include those of car manufacturers such as BMW, Ferrari, Honda, and McLaren. A constructor usually has two cars, and two drivers usually race for each constructor.

A driver (center) and his team's mechanics talk about their car's performance.

World Championships

There are **rankings** for both drivers and teams throughout the racing season. The top 8 finishers in each Grand Prix race score points toward both the Drivers' World Championship and the Constructors' World Championship. The list on page 19 shows how the points are given out.

Grand Prix Point System

1st place	10 points
2nd place	8 points
3rd place	6 points
4th place	5 points
5th place	4 points
6th place	3 points
7th place	2 points
8th place	1 point

A constructor earns points for both of its drivers and cars. At the end of the season, the driver with the most points is declared Drivers' World Champion. The constructor with the most points is the Constructors' World Champion.

You Do the Math

Tallying the Points

The table shows the points earned by 3 drivers in each of 7 races. Use the table to answer the questions.

Points Earned by 3 Drivers in 7 Races			
Race	Driver A	Driver B	Driver C
1	10	8	5
2	8	10	5
3	8	5	10
4	10	6	8
5	8	10	6
6	10	8	6
7	8	6	3

1. At the end of 7 races, how many total points does each driver have?
2. Which driver has the most first place finishes?

The Fuel

Although F1 cars are highly specialized machines, they run on fuel that is very similar to regular gasoline. Each team develops its own fuel blend designed to make the team's cars run best.

Fueling Up: The Pit Stop

During a race, a car will need more fuel, will need to have its tires changed, and may need mechanical adjustments. The car has to pull off into a special area on one side of the track for a pit stop. The car stops in

A pit crew can refuel a car and change its tires in as little as 7 seconds.

an exact position in the pit, so that team members can very quickly refuel it, change the tires, and do anything else the car needs. Every second counts because when the car is in the pit, it's not on the track. Usually, team members need between 7 and 20 seconds before the car is ready to leave the pit and get back to racing.

An F1 car crosses the finish line to win a Grand Prix race.

How Much Fuel Do We Need?

F1 race cars use a lot of fuel. In fact, many F1 cars get only about 4 miles per gallon. A full tank means a heavier and slower car, so teams have to decide how much fuel they will start the race with. Should they start with a tank that is one-third full to get ahead right away? Or will starting with only that much fuel mean an extra pit stop for refueling, which will cost time? Answering questions like these are all part of the race strategy. Think about these questions about refueling?

1. F1 cars can usually be refueled at a rate of 3 gallons per second. If the pit crew adds 30 gallons of fuel to a car, how long will refueling take?

2. Most F1 cars use about 55 gallons of fuel in every race. If a car used that much fuel and got 4 miles per gallon, how far did it travel in the race?

3. If an F1 car begins a race with 28 gallons of fuel and needs 55 gallons to complete the race, how much more fuel will it need during a pit stop?

The Tires

Racing tires are made from very soft rubber that gives the best grip on the track. The tires wear out quickly, though, usually lasting only 125 miles at most. In comparison, regular car tires can often last 20,000–30,000 miles or more.

F1 race teams use a careful strategy to decide which tires to use in a race. If it is raining at the start of the race, they will likely put wet-weather tires on the car. With such tires, the car can't go quite as fast, but it is less likely to aquaplane (slide across the track out of control) on a wet track.

Cars need wet-weather tires for racing in the rain.

If the weather improves, then when the tires are changed at a pit stop, the team might switch to softer tires. These tires are smoother than the all-weather ones and can run the fastest.

Things Will Go Wrong

Sometimes things go wrong during a race, and a car is unable to finish. Even though the team has prepared the car and thought carefully about race strategy, the car can have mechanical problems, or it may be in an accident. People who follow F1 racing talk about a team's reliability. Measuring a team's reliability involves comparing how many races the team completed with how many races the team entered. Often a team's reliability is expressed as a percent. Every team wants to complete as high a percent as possible of the races it enters.

You Do the Math

Looking at Reliability

The bar graph shows the reliability of five F1 teams. Use the graph to answer the questions.

1. Which team has the highest level of reliability?

2. Which team has the lowest level of reliability?

3. Which teams have at least 75 percent reliability or more?

4. Did any team have less than 50 percent reliability?

F1 Team Reliability

Teams — TEAM A, TEAM B, TEAM C, TEAM D, TEAM E

Percent: 0 10 20 30 40 50 60 70 80 90 100

How's My Driving?

Almost every part of a Formula One race is studied mathematically by a race team—tires, fuel, when to make a pit stop. However, there are some things that can't be planned. These include an unexpected change in the weather or a mistake by the driver. Even the most skilled and experienced drivers are human and can make mistakes.

Race Results

During a race, spectators can watch a number of things. They can see which driver is ahead of the other drivers and which cars are in the pit. If clouds are rolling in, they can see who is changing to rain tires and who is leaving the faster smooth tires on, hoping that the rain will hold off until after the race is finished.

The top-three finishers on the podium after an F1 race.

Seeing the skill of the drivers is, for most people, probably the best part of watching a race. The drivers take **hairpin turns** at high speed and may need to react quickly to steer around an accident that's just happened in front of them. Every driver wants to be standing on the podium (platform) at the end of the race, when medals are given to the drivers who finished in first, second, and third place.

Hairpin turns are common on F1 tracks.

Numbers on the Drivers

When you're driving an expensive race car and you have an entire team of people backing you up, you need to be skilled. Records are kept on how drivers perform in every race. How often does a driver run the fastest lap or step to the podium to accept a medal? The graph shows data for four drivers. Use the graph to answer the questions.

1. Which driver had the most podium appearances?

2. Which driver had the highest number of fastest laps?

Fastest Laps — Podium Appearances

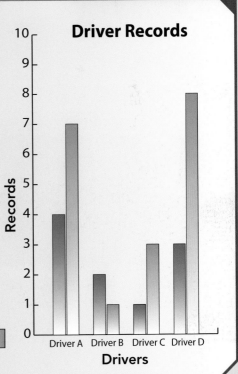

Driver Records

(Records vs. Drivers: Driver A, Driver B, Driver C, Driver D)

Driver Training

Imagine sitting in the cramped **cockpit** of a Formula One race car for 2 hours. There's no room to move. The temperature is usually high, so drivers may sweat a great deal. F1 drivers drink a lot of water before a race, so they won't suffer from **dehydration**. Many people think that driving in an F1 race is as demanding as running a marathon.

F1 drivers are well-trained athletes. They keep in shape by running, swimming, cycling, or even roller blading. They also need to build strong neck muscles. These muscles must support their head and a heavy helmet as their body shifts position when they take sharp turns at high speed.

An F1 driver needs to be in top physical condition.

A Driver's Day

What is a typical day like for F1 drivers? The table on page 27 shows one driver's typical schedule for a day.

Driver's Daily Schedule

Time	Activity
7:00 A.M.	Work out with personal trainer. Run. Ride exercise bike.
9:00 A.M.	Drive laps with managers in a regular car. Identify hairpin turns and other curves in the track. Discuss driving strategy.
9:45 A.M.	On the track in the race car. Test new tires.
10:15 A.M.	Into the pit. Car goes up on air jacks to check tires. Engineer reviews lap times.
10:25 A.M.	Drive more laps. Focus on taking the curves.
11:20 A.M.	Spun out. Into the pit for a check.
11:45 A.M.	Back on the track. Drive more laps. Try for better lap times.
12:30 P.M.	Into the pit. Tires checked and changed.
1:00 P.M.	Lunch.
1:30 P.M.	Continue driving laps. Focus on time.
2:30 P.M.	Into the pit. Car is checked. Meet with engineers and managers to review time data.
3:00 P.M.	Back on the track. Test lap time with half load of fuel.
3:45 P.M.	Into the pit. Review data with team.
5:30 P.M.	Work out with personal trainer. Swim until 7:30 P.M.

You Do the Math

How Much Time?

Use the driver's daily schedule to answer the questions.

1. How much time does the driver spend exercising and working out with a personal trainer?
2. What time does the driver first start using his race car?
3. How much time is spent driving laps after lunch?

If You Want to Be a Race Car Driver

Racing is a demanding sport. Race car drivers need to be in excellent physical condition. They should also understand how car engines work and how such things as type of tires can affect a car's performance.

Although auto racing doesn't require a college education, knowledge of math and science are important. Drivers need to know math to understand the analysis of data that is so important to a winning race strategy. Knowledge of science principles will also help drivers understand such things as the forces acting on a car when, for example, it takes a sharp turn at high speed.

There are racing schools that offer driver training. Nearly all race car drivers begin by getting experience in amateur races while they develop their skills.

There is also more to racing than driving the car. A race car driver is a member of a team. The driver must be able to communicate and work effectively with other people.

Answer Key

Pages 4-5: Racing and Math:
1. Texas Motor Speedway: 196 mph. **2.** Las Vegas Motor Speedway: 185 mph. **3.** 11 mph (196 − 185 = 11). **4.** 5 mph (196 − 191 = 5).

Pages 6-7: Track Design:
1. Martinsville, 65,000; Kansas City, 82,000; Dover, 140,000; Charlotte, 165,000; Daytona Beach, 168,000; Indianapolis, 250,000. **2.** Daytona Beach and Indianapolis. **3.** 2 miles (2.5 − 0.5 = 2). **4.** 115,000 seats (250,000 − 135,000 = 115,000).

Pages 8-9: Drag Racing:
1. Tran had the shortest elapsed time (by 0.26 seconds). Steph had the fastest speed (by 0.03 mph). Tran is the winner because he had the shorter elapsed time. **2.** Ed lost the race. The difference between his elapsed time and Jason's elapsed time is 1.50 seconds (9.18 − 7.68 = 1.50).

Pages 10-11: E.T. Racing:
1. 12 seconds (12 + 10 + 14 = 36; 36 ÷ 3 = 12). **2.** 15.5 seconds (14.5 + 16 + 16 = 46.5; 46.5 ÷ 3 = 15.5).

Pages 12-13: Go as Fast as You Can!:
1. Driver B with 9 race wins. **2.** Driver A with 11 pole starts. **3.** Driver B won 8 more races than Driver D (9 − 1 = 8). **4.** Driver D won 3 more pole starts than Driver B (4 − 1 = 3).

Pages 14-15: NASCAR: Winning the Championship:
1. Driver A: 596 points; Driver B: 547 points; Driver C: 740 points; Driver D: 622 points. **2.** 144 points (740 − 596 = 144). **3.** Driver B. **4.** Driver C, with 30 bonus points (5 + 10 + 5 + 10 = 30). **5.** Driver C (740), Driver D (622), Driver A (596), Driver B (547).

Pages 16-17: Formula One:
1. NASCAR tracks are oval. Formula One tracks are irregularly shaped road courses. **2.** NASCAR cars look like road cars. Formula One cars have long noses, huge tires, and wing-like parts. **3.** Possible answers: Drivers get points depending on the order in which they finish. Teams support each driver. Drivers compete all season to win the championship.

Pages 18-19: F1: The Driver and His Team:
1. Driver A: 62 points; Driver B: 53 points; Driver C: 43 points. **2.** Driver A. Finishing first is worth 10 points. Driver A got 10 points 3 times, Driver B twice, and Driver C once.

Pages 20-21: The Fuel:
1. 10 seconds (30 ÷ 3 = 10). **2.** 220 miles (55 x 4 = 220). **3.** 27 gallons (55 − 28 = 27).

Pages 22-23: The Tires:
1. Team C (85%). **2.** Team D (55%). **3.** Team A (80%) and Team C (85%). **4.** No, because the lowest reliability is 55%.

Pages 24-25: How's My Driving?:
1. Driver D had the most podium appearances (8). **2.** Driver A had the highest number of fastest laps (4).

Pages 26-27: Driver Training:
1. 4 hours (2 hours from 7:00 A.M. to 9:00 A.M. plus 2 hours from 5:30 P.M. to 7:30 P.M.). **2.** 9:45 A.M. **3.** 1 hour, 45 minutes (1 hour from 1:30 P.M. to 2:30 P.M. plus 45 minutes from 3:00 P.M. to 3:45 P.M.).

Glossary

analyze—To examine or study.

average—The sum of a group of numbers divided by the quantity of numbers in the group; also called the mean.

bar graph—A graph that uses bars to show data.

calculate—To figure out the exact answer to a problem.

cockpit—Where the driver sits and the controls are located inside a race car.

data—Information.

dehydration—A large loss of water from the body, which can cause medical problems.

difference—The amount by which one number is greater than another number.

elapsed time—The amount of time that has gone by since the start of an event.

hairpin turn—A sharp, U-shaped turn that has a shape similar to a hairpin.

pit stop—A stop a driver makes during a race in an area (pit) alongside the track, where members of the driver's team may refuel the car, change tires, and do other maintenance.

pole position—The starting position in a race on an oval track that is closest to the inside of the track.

qualifying time—The fastest time that each race car goes once around the track before a race.

ranking—A listing in order, often from greatest to least.

stock car—A regular car that has been changed for racing.

sum—The answer when two or more numbers are added together.

Venn diagram—A diagram that has two circles that may overlap and that shows the relationships among sets of things.

To Learn More

Read these books:

Cavin, Curt. *Race Day! The Fastest Show on Earth*. Excelsior, Minn.: Tradition Books, 2003.

Franks, Katie. *I Want to Be a Race Car Driver*. New York: Rosen Publishing, 2007.

Stewart, Mark, and Mike Kennedy. *NASCAR in the Driver's Seat*. Minneapolis: Lerner Publishing Group, 2008.

West, David. *Race Car Drivers*. New York: Rosen Publishing, 2008.

Look up these Web sites:

Formula One Official Website
http://www.formula1.com

National Association for Stock Car Auto Racing (NASCAR)
http://www.nascar.com

National Hot Rod Association
http://www.nhra.com

Key Internet search terms:

automobile racing, drag racing, Formula One, NASCAR, stock car racing

Index

About the Author

Sheri L. Arroyo has a master of arts degree in education. She has been an elementary school teacher in San Diego, California, for more than twenty years and has taught third grade for the past thirteen years.